BUTTERFLIES SNOWBIRDS  PASSIONS

A CHAPBOOK OF POEMS and FANTASIES

RONALD P. FELDHEIM

BUTTERFLIES SNOWBIRDS AND PASSIONS: A Chapbook of Poems and Fantasies
Copyright © 2021 Ronald P. Feldheim All rights reserved.

All rights reserved. No part of this book may be reproduced or used in any manner without written permission of the copyright owner except for the use of quotations in a book review.

Cover Design, Typography & Production by Hallard Press LLC/John W Prince
Cover & Interior Images: AdobeStock

Published by Hallard Press LLC.
www.HallardPress.com   Info@HallardPress.com   352-234-6099
Bulk copies of this book can be ordered at Info@HallardPress.com

Publisher's Cataloging-in-Publication data

Names: Feldheim, Ronald P., author.
Title: Butterflies , snowbirds , and passions : a chapbook of poems and fantasies / Ronald P. Feldheim.
Description: The Villages, FL: Hallard Press, LLC, 2021.
Identifiers: LCCN: 2021924685 | ISBN: 978-1-951188-39-9
Subjects: LCSH American poetry--21st century. | Nature poetry. | BISAC POETRY / American / General | POETRY / Subjects & Themes / Inspirational & Religious | POETRY / Subjects & Themes / Nature
Classification: LCC PS3606.E3856 B98 2021 | DDC 811.54--dc23

Typography
Titles: Hypatia Sans Pro Light
Body Type: Novarese Bk BT Regular

Printed in the United States of America

ISBN: (Paperback) 978-1-951188-39-9

Ronald P. Feldheim

CHAPBOOK

A chapbook is a small publication, often poetry. In early modern Europe a chapbook was a type of printed street literature.

A chapbook excerpts the general aesthetic of the author, while allowing a little leeway for them to explore either something new, like style or form, or topic that might not fill a book.

The term "chapbook" for this type of literature was coined in the 19th century. The corresponding French term is *bibliothèque bleue* (blue library) because they were often wrapped in cheap blue paper that was usually reserved as a wrapping for sugar.

I'm sentimental, yes that's true,
I owe my rules, to all of you.
There's Anita & Peter,
There's Bonnie & Mardy,
There's Clare & Ralph,
There's Tracy & Sandi,
There's Ryan & Jerry,
There's Debbie & Harry,
There's Jenny, Thedda & Paul
There's for others Rebecca & John.
I'm delighted to see you here
To celebrate my added year.

Perhaps you might put this in
  some book,
So in future years, when on its
    pages you look,
It will serve to recall this day of
    mine,
April 5th, 1979   Love
                    Mother
                    Nana

Ronald P. Feldheim

DEDICATION

I dedicate this book in memory of Nana, Shirley LeNoble, the original poet in my family. Her poetry, which she composed and read for numerous family gatherings, inspired me to write my first poem.

I also dedicate this work to my life partner, Nancy Kraemer. Her own poetry, applied with a dose of feminine wiles, brought us together to begin what has turned into a wondrous adventure.

TABLE OF CONTENTS

INTRODUCTION	1
SPIRITUALITY	5
Butterflies and Sailing Ships	7
A Psalm Of Home	8
The Call	10
Atonement: I Sing	12
Cool Stones	15
NATURE	17
The Gecko	19
Soaring	20
Snowbirds	22
Asymmetry	24
Haiku	26
An Aha Moment	29
EMOTION	31
Nana	32
Heartsong	34
How Can I Not Rise?	35
Safe	37
Lonely Place	38
September Mourning	41
Cycles	42
A Teardrop	44
Driving To The Sun	45

MIRABILE	47
Reflection	48
Passion	50
And Not To Yield	51
Sometimes You Want To Wallow in Your Sadness .	52
POEMS FROM THE TIME OF COVID	57
At Least The Birds Are Still Flying Free	58
Now Or Then	61
Give Me a Poem	62
ACKNOWLEDGEMENTS	64
MEET THE AUTHOR	65

Ronald P. Feldheim

INTRODUCTION

This little booklet is a collection of some of my favorite compositions. I wrote them over a long span of years, and they reveal several facets of my individuality. The discerning reader might notice little lessons in some of these works.

I generally write only when some event inspires me, or when I have something to say. Sometimes a song will catch my fancy, and I'll use the rhythm to compose an entirely new poem.

Composing haiku began as an exercise while travelling extensively for work. I contrived to paint word pictures of my experiences to share with my girlfriend as I moved around solo from place to place.

Cycles was written as self-therapy one day while I drove to a meeting, notepad lying on the passenger's seat. I intentionally wrote two poems at the same time. One laid out my emotional problem, progressed to reveal the turmoil it brought, and concluded with a hopeful understanding of my improved state of mind. The second poem was a tight narrative drumbeat to the first, which seemed to require this companion piece. It reminds me of the chorus in a Greek drama. I am not aware of any other poems structured this way, and don't know where the idea came from.

I have gathered these writings into three general categories. **Spirituality** includes my religious practice as a Jew, as well as my connection to the higher-vibrational realm of spirit. **Nature** reflects my life-long passion for being out in the natural world, studying it, and understanding it. **Emotion** includes poems about love, desire, sadness, joy, and other feelings.

As an addendum I have added some new works which I wrote from quarantine.

Ron

Ronald P. Feldheim

Ronald P. Feldheim

SPIRITUALITY

Ronald P. Feldheim

BUTTERFLIES AND SAILING SHIPS

Butterflies and sailing ships fly freely in the breeze,
Captured heartstrings trailing in their wake.
Giving rise to wistful songs and fantasies, they tease
A longing for our earthly bonds to break.

Butterflies and sailing ships, propelled like autumn leaves;
Racing swiftly, kindred spirits, they.
Yet dying winds will leave a ship imbedded in the seas.
And gales will tumble butterflies astray.

Butterflies and sailing ships, deceivingly, they seem
Symbolic of elusive joy sustained.
Pastoral and nautical, illusions of a dream:
From quiet depths are joy, and peace, attained.

We are free to fly at will, or race before the storm.
Tranquility and freedom are our well-spring and our form.
As the butterfly, from chrysalis, spreads wings to dry and warm,
So **we** shrug off shrouds and Light restores our norm.

A PSALM OF HOME*

How do I lift up my eyes to the mountains?
Mountains are far from this land where I dwell.
How shall I know the source of my help?
Can the song of the psalmist be my song as well?

My help comes while gazing across ocean's reaches;
From wave crests reflecting the dazzle of day.
I gain peace of mind during dusk, walking beaches.
The sibilant surf speaks of God on my way.

Watching a sunrise I sense my soul lighten.
The Lord in his Glory has given this day.
Yet sky's painted sunsets enliven, and brighten.
A curtain call prelude of Moon, Milky Way.

Ronald P. Feldheim

The taste of a mango is true hint of Heaven.
Perfume from orchards of orange sublime.
The fruits of the land number seven times seven.
The season for harvest is most any time.

A thousand ibises fill me with pleasure.
A lone painted bunting brings joy as Divine.
Warbler, eagle, hummingbird: treasures.
By glade, sea or hammock I drink in God's sign.

Night-blooming jasmine is wafted on bay breeze.
Laughter of children by day fills the air.
Bayscapes so splendid a hard heart must find ease.
Where is my help? It is found everywhere.

*inspired by Psalm 121

THE CALL*

It pierces me, O Lord, it pierces me!
The call of the *shofar* grips my heart,
A lance of sound tipped by mystery and awe.
My breath catches in my throat.
Shame and joy, love and dread
Flood out of my suddenly awakened spirit,
Wash over me as a tide.

TEKIAH!
Have I been asleep?
I am suddenly sharply awake, alert.

TERUAH!
What have I been doing?
Have I grown since last year?
Am I ready for judgement?

SHEVARIM!
H*ineni*, O Lord. I am here.
I accept my faults, and vow to improve.
I dedicate my merits to Your service.
I will heal the world, *Tikkun Olam*,
One action at a time, one person at a time.
I will heal myself, *Tikkun Middot*,
One day at a time.

TEKIAH GEDOLAH!
The final blast thrills me to my depths,
Leaves me awash in joy,
And hope.

It pierces me, O Lord, it pierces me.
And in that eternal moment I am transformed.
I am ready.

*for Rosh Hashanah

ATONEMENT: I SING*

I sing the joy of cleansing prayer,
The inner work that lays me bare.
Before the Loving Light I stand,
My sins illumined should I dare.

I sing.

I sing of loss, I sing of gain,
The blanching of the hidden stain,
The purifying of my heart.
"Empty, empty" my refrain.

I sing.

I sing of old, I sing of new.
This emptied vessel will renew,
To build again from finer stuff
A nearer image, Lord, of You.

I sing!

Ronald P. Feldheim

I view myself as if apart:
This freshly reconstructed heart.
A different imperfection found.
Another change, another start.

I SING!

So it goes from year to year,
A little here, a little there.
O Lord, you beckon, call my name.
Hineni, Lord, for I am near.

I am the song.

*for Yom Kippur

Butterflies, Snowbirds, and Passions: Poems and Fantasies

Ronald P. Feldheim

COOL STONES

The cool stones beckoned,
Those ancient cool stones.
They spoke of millions of prayers.
They remember thousands of generations.
The cool stones beckoned, and I was ready.

We stepped forward, my rabbi and I.
Why did the others stay back?
I stepped forward with my rabbi
And self-consciously followed his lead.

I placed my hands and bowed my head against the cool stone.
The focus of ages, those cool stones.
Then prayers, millions of prayers, flowed into me from this
  living stone.
I trembled as thoughts and voices flooded into me,
Thoughts and voices and faces beyond count, all at once,
  right there.
"Next year in Jerusalem," at those cool stones.
And screams of anguish, at those cool stones.
It seemed more than I could bear, more than I could bear.
There, where I stood with my hands and bowed head
  against the cool stone.

How can I explain the Light that appeared at that moment?
A column of Light, stretching from God to me! Here. By
  the stones.

I could sense God's presence, see God's attendants.
Trembling, I came to realize that I was in the spotlight.
I had God's ear! A direct link.
How can I possibly explain?

I knew what to ask for. There was no question.
Lord God Almighty, I prayed. Creator of the Universe, I
  pleaded.
Shalom, I begged. S*halom*!
Peace for Israel, peace for the Middle East, peace for all
  nations.
I prayed with every fiber of my being. There, in the spotlight.
God gave me a chance to plead my case, there, by the
  cool stones.
I prayed, as if the world depended upon **me.**
Then the eternal moment was over, and I turned to leave.
I stayed behind the others, unable to speak.
The world looked blurred and felt unsteady.

I left that place but my heart is tethered there yet.
At times, unexpectedly, it tugs me back, and I weep then.
For even now, EVEN NOW, I remember.
Lord, can a hopeful heart make a difference?
I plead again: another day of peace, and another, and
  another...

I remember those cool stones.

Ronald P. Feldheim

NATURE

Butterflies, Snowbirds, and Passions: Poems and Fantasies

Ronald P. Feldheim

THE GECKO

There's a gecko in my bathroom.
It arrived not long ago.
I found it when I moved the scale
That measures **HIGH** or ʟᴏᴡ.
It gave me quite a startle,
Yet I had to stop and think:
Should I catch it?
        Kill it?
               Leave it be?
Then it gave a little slink.

There's a gecko in my bathroom.
It must be finding food.
It looks at me, it cocks its head,
And brightens up my mood.
This creature's such a cutie
I can't chase it away.
I anticipate it showing
When I take my nightly weigh.

There's a gecko in my bathroom.
Well, maybe it has left.
I haven't seen it lately
And I feel a bit bereft.
I hope that it is happy,
If such a thing can be.
I sure miss that little fella,
Or, maybe he's a she.

SOARING

Swooping low over the sawgrass
Sliding left for a close pass over star-like lilies
From this vantage the world appears as a prickly pale-
  green sea
I sneak a peek backward under my outstretched right arm
The nearer blades are blurred by my speed
The more distant blades become blurred as they merge
  into this sea of grass
Sparkling reflections of the sun cause me to squint

Far ahead the crown of a cypress dome begins to emerge:
An island in the ocean
Its separate feathery entities not yet apparent

I hear the bell-song of Red-winged Blackbirds and turn in
  their direction
There they are, resting on blades that bow under their weight
I slow and glide directly over them
Their red-and yellow epaulets contrast starkly
With the ebony of the males' feathers
The lighter mottling of the females'

Now I skirt a small hardwood hammock
A kettle of Turkey Vultures is fringed by a few Black Vultures
The wait is apparently over as individuals drop out of the flock
To disappear beneath the canopy

Ronald P. Feldheim

Big cypresses loom ahead
I bank right to parallel the contours of the island
The white snowflakes clinging to the branches
Resolve into scimitar-billed Ibises, gray-headed Wood
  Storks, Snowy Egrets
A dozen Roseate Spoonbills glide toward the shallows
A young alligator swims slowly along shore
On the bank a stately Great Egret struggles with a
  Coachwhip
Three feet of tail thrashing futilely against the stout yellow
  bill
The snake's head deep in the bird's gullet
Soft-shell Turtles snorkel among Flag and Pickerel Weed
Red-bellied Turtles sun three-deep on a floating log
An Osprey heads for a high snag
A bass carried like a torpedo in its talons

I veer away and up, up, up
I fly under a solitary black-gray cloud
Its cooling shower rolling off my skin, wetting my hair
I dry almost as quickly, as I find a thermal current and ride
  toward the sun
Gazing out over the glorious landscape spiraling below

If only...

SNOWBIRDS

As I was leaving Miami Beach the other day, I witnessed the unlikely combination of a Magnificent Frigate Bird riding the thermals alongside the Julia Tuttle Causeway in the company of two Turkey Vultures. Today, in the same place, I saw another Frigate Bird circling with a Turkey Vulture. Wondering if they were the same birds I saw last time, I tried to imagine how the sea bird and the land scavenger paired up.

"Hey, Turkey Vulture."

"Yeah?"

"Where are we?"

"Georgia."

"That's what I thought. You sure?"

"'Smy third trip. Where you headed, Miami?"

"Miami Beach. You?"

"Miami."

"You going to the old courthouse downtown?"

"Well, that's where I sleep at night. Once the morning warms up a little, I join the Mount Trashmore tour. The garbage dumps are all around South Florida."

"Yuck!"

"What 'yuck'?"

"That's disgusting!"

"There's good eats at the dumps."

"Like I said, 'yuck'."

"Whatta you eat, pretty boy?"

"Fish."

"I eat dead stuff."

"The fish I catch are dead soon enough."

"I eat fish, when I can get 'em."

"I've got this great fishing spot, right by this beautiful causeway."

"You mean where they're building that ugly high rise?"

"That's the one. Sometimes fishermen leave dead fish behind. People toss trash there, too. You ought to come join me, check it out."

"Don't mind if I do. I might bring my girlfriend along."

"You have a girlfriend?"

"She says we're just friends. But last year, when we got to Miami, we... you know."

"Yeah. There's this chick I've had my eye on."

"Love Miami."

"Great town, great town."

ASYMMETRY

A-symmetry
A-symmetry
A-symmetry
Blaming it for everything

Why do things bunch up together?
Why do things happen at once?
We have to choose what to go to
The rest we have to say no.

Sometimes there's nothing planned
And sometimes everything bunches together
Usually it's like this:
On Saturdays I go to Temple in the morning and maybe go out at night
But sometimes it's something like this:
It's *Shevuot* eve dinner and study with one set of friends
While at the same time it's *Havurah* night with another set of friends
And it's the same day I have go into work to do an upgrade
And it's the same afternoon my friends invited me to join them when they become citizens

A-symmetry
A-symmetry
A-symmetry
Blaming it for everything

Ronald P. Feldheim

It all goes back to the Big Bang
Light burst out
And if it burst out evenly it would have created a Universe
full of diffuse light and nothing more
But the light came out unevenly
More in some directions
Less in others
That created eddies and swirls
And the eddies and swirls bumped into each other
And that slowed some of them down
So that out of the light came matter
The matter created eddies and swirls
They bumped into each other
And out of those came galaxies
And eventually solar systems
And eventually Earth

A-symmetry
A-symmetry
A-symmetry
Blaming it for everything

Here in the course of existence
There are wrinkles
Events gather in between the wrinkles
So sometimes there is nothing going on
And sometimes everything bunches up together
And that's why I can't go to my friends' citizen swearing-in ceremony

HAIKU

Miami Beach 9/02:
rootbound, transplanted
first tentative petals open
bee finds treat, sips long

crests chase troughs shoreward
huddled figure wrapped in robe
aging eyes ageless

softness envelops
fragile dreams search unmapped bounds
pulses galloping

above Charleston 9/12/02:
puffs float on milk sea
high blue dome bears silver stacks
sun illumines all

Miami Beach 9/18/02*:
pale moon over sea
dying sun hides behind clouds
frenzied world pauses

sands shift under foot
waves break, light breeze stirs sea oats
peaceful joy swells heart

cloud caps catch last light
eastward sky brightens like dawn
day succumbs to night

Thomasville, GA 9/25/02
stately oaks command
limbs reach to gather-in homes
calm sentries on guard

Miami Beach 10/18/02
Chill breeze welcomes day
Diving terns cry as gulls chase
Sundrop peeks at sky

Simpsonwood 11/3/02
rainbow leaves drift down
trees screen mist-layered river
wary doe lifts head

Anderson, SC 1/31/03
pointillist mist falls
chill penetrates all layers
warm home is remote

Andalusia, AL 2/4/03
brown fields undulate
skeleton trees stand in lake
clouds play while moon beams

Charleston, SC 3/12/03
blossoms drape tall homes
storied walls hug perfumed lanes
gardens dance within

Charleston, SC 3/19/03
horses draw tourists
history dwells in city's soul
old spirits live on

Augusta, GA 6/4/03
river flows below
trestled tracks meet levee heights
perfumes waft on wind

Miami Beach 1/1/13
Silver crests beckon.
Distant shores stand forlornly,
Waiting my return.

Golden flower nods.
Busy tender drinks her fill.
Honey cake to follow.

*This haiku triplet was aired by Rick Steves on his national radio show, and posted to his website.

Ronald P. Feldheim

AN AHA MOMENT

Tonight I solved a mystery
A riddle of the ages
It came to me while listening to
The wisdom of the sages

The History Channel showed me
Perfect spirals cut in stone
They're found around the globe, they said
Where petroglyphs are known

They said that it was aliens
On vortex wormhole missions
Remembered by the ancient folks
In stony compositions

Others profess it represents
The chaos of creation
The whirls and swirls of energy
That led to Earth's formation

But I solved what they really are
An ancient sort of cookbook
This dish once found in old Cathay
Now everywhere you look

My dinner was the lucky key
Watching TV as I ate
They're pictures of the perfect way
TO SERVE SPAGHETTI ON A PLATE!

Ronald P. Feldheim

EMOTION

NANA

She was Shirley to some folks but Nana to me.
Nanas have a special place in little grandkids' lives.
Her bright thread is woven into the fabric of my earliest
  memories.
I celebrate her wondrous spirit, her determined
  independence;
Giving and caring, loving and sharing.
That's what she means to me.

I remember holiday dinners with family members I hardly
  knew.
I remember chopped liver, oh, such a treat,
And eggplant relish delivered in person, the vinegary
  aroma drawing stares on the bus.
There were nights we stayed up late, talking, just us two.
And cookies, wonderful cookies.
These are the things Nana means to me.

There was inner strength in great measure,
And an equal portion of stubbornness.
These are what got her through the tough times.
A will, a determination, to enjoy life and participate in it.
What admiration these qualities drew.
All these and more are what Nana means to me.

Ronald P. Feldheim

Knitting, knitting, knitting, always knitting, with gifts of
  sweaters.
And dancing, how she LOVED to dance.
Her distinctive sharp gravelly voice that I struggle to still
  hear, with funny words like kukle-mukle and hoity-toity.

Always involved with family, she knitted the loose ends
  together as they became unraveled.
So many, many ways did Nana show her love.
That is what she means to me.

Nana, I love you.

HEARTSONG*

Our love, our love is our passage free
It is faith for you; it is hope for me.
We can soar on wings, over rainbows see.
When our hearts sing the song of our glory.

Love, love is our heart's content.
It's our artist's palette, the lives we've spent.
Our light will shine 'cross the firmament.
When our heart sings the song of our glory.

Our love, our love is our symphony.
It's the singular note in our harmony;
The golden hue on the autumn tree,
When our heart sings the song of our glory.

Our love, our love is the tie that binds.
It's the bridge of souls as our lives unwind;
The forge that links in our chain of minds,
When our heart sings the song of our glory.

inspired by the song Greensleeves

Ronald P. Feldheim

HOW CAN I NOT RISE?*

'Though I sprawl in the mud,
'Though I beseech the Almighty in vain,
'Though I am in utter despair,
    How can I not rise?

'Though my heart is broken,
'Though my family is lost,
'Though my neighbors are gone,
    How can I not rise?

'Though my whole body aches,
'Though I am starving and have no work,
'Though war is raging all around,
    How can I not rise?

Because the sky brightens with the new dawn, I rise.
Because a sparrow chirps from a broken branch, I rise.
Because a breeze cools my face, I rise.
Because as long as breath fills my lungs I **must** rise.

    I must.

*inspired by the sculpture, How Can I Rise? by Norbert Shamuyarira from Chinoyl, Zimbabwe

Butterflies, Snowbirds, and Passions: Poems and Fantasies

Ronald P. Feldheim

SAFE

Outside, driven flecks, drifted flakes.
Milky swirls, obscuring, scouring, layering.
Forceful fingers explore for hidden entrances.
Moans and whistles and howls emitted in protest.
Evergreens lean away from relentless gales,
Weighted with frozen deposits,
Shaking to free themselves to no avail.

Inside, warmth from hearth and hearts.
Wood and glass separating,
Protecting the life within from the life without.
A cocoon, a capsule;
All within comfortable and secure.
Daily routines, happy talk, quiet activities.

Outside, a growing darkness to hide the frigid forces
Pummeling the land since before dawn.

Inside, a growing uneasiness well-hidden.
Will the darkness and the cold find their way in?

LONELY PLACE

For the past fifteen minutes he has been extracting the remains of lunch, the plastic toothpick from his two-inch pocketknife moving rhythmically from tooth to tooth. It was an almost futile attempt to remain awake, let alone alert. The squeal of the windshield wipers passed the annoying stage miles ago. He resented having to drive thirty miles for dinner at the end of a long, frustrating day for another meal eaten alone. What kind of town doesn't even have a place to eat dinner? He was hoping he could find the restaurant suggested by his customer. The attractive rolling hills of central Georgia disappeared in the wet darkness, limited to a too-short landing strip of reflectors in the cars headlights. He dodged the reflected high-beams of yet another jacked-up pick-up coming up on his tail. Isn't there a single considerate driver on the road? The only saving grace was that he had made this same drive to a different restaurant in this distant town last night. He would manage. Didn't he always? A swelling cloud bank was brushing the tree tops, while ahead, an orange glow highlighted either ground fog or smoke. It made him nervous. He daydreamed.

He imagined writing a novel, with himself as the central character. It would open with an attention-getting sentence about driving down a lonely highway at night:

Ronald P. Feldheim

For the past fifteen minutes he has been extracting the remains of lunch, the plastic toothpick from his two-inch pocketknife moving rhythmically from tooth to tooth. It was an almost futile attempt to remain awake, let alone alert. The squeal of the windshield wipers passed the annoying stage miles ago. He resented having to drive thirty miles for dinner at the end of a long, frustrating day for another meal eaten alone. What kind of town doesn't even have a place to eat dinner? He was hoping he could find the restaurant suggested by his customer. The attractive rolling hills of central Georgia disappeared in the wet darkness, limited to a too-short landing strip of reflectors in the cars headlights. He dodged the reflected high-beams of yet another jacked-up pick-up coming up on his tail. Isn't there a single considerate driver on the road? The only saving grace was that he had made this same drive to a different restaurant in this distant town last night. He would manage. Didn't he always? A swelling cloud bank was brushing the tree tops, while ahead, an orange glow highlighted either ground fog or smoke. It made him nervous. He daydreamed.

He imagined writing a novel, with himself as the central character. It would open with an attention-getting sentence about driving down a lonely highway at night:

For the past fifteen minutes he has been extracting the remains of lunch, the plastic toothpick from his two-inch pocketknife moving rhythmically from tooth to tooth. It was an almost futile attempt to remain awake, let alone alert. The squeal of the windshield wipers passed the annoying stage miles ago. He resented having to drive thirty miles for dinner at the end of a long, frustrating day for another meal eaten alone. What kind of town doesn't even have a place to eat dinner? He was hoping he could find the restaurant suggested by his customer. The attractive rolling hills of central Georgia disappeared in the wet darkness, limited to a too-short landing strip of reflectors in the cars headlights. He dodged the reflected high-beams of yet another jacked-up pick-up coming up on his tail. Isn't there a single considerate driver on the road? The only saving grace was that he had made this same drive to a different restaurant in this distant town last night. He would manage. Didn't he always? A swelling cloud bank was brushing the tree tops, while ahead, an orange glow highlighted either ground fog or smoke. It made him nervous. He daydreamed.

He imagined writing a novel, with himself as the central character. It would open with an attention-getting sentence about driving down a lonely highway at night:

For the past fifteen minutes he has been extracting the remains of lunch, the plastic toothpick from his two-inch pocketknife moving rhythmically from tooth to tooth. It was an almost futile attempt to remain

Ronald P. Feldheim

SEPTEMBER MOURNING*

Arise, arise, O ye innocents of God;
Arise, and leave your beds of pain.
His tears have filled a stream to follow through his gates.
Her arms will comfort and sustain.

Arise, arise, O ye families and ye friends;
Arise to face the coming dawn.
That hope and promise now can never come to pass.
In you the memories live on.

Arise, arise, all ye tremulous and bowed,
Arise, make straight your bended knee.
Through your anguish lift your face and lift your heart.
In faith, God's promise is for thee.

a response to the September 11th terrorist attacks, inspired by A Sparrow Song *by Richard Fariña*

CYCLES

panoply of ancient lives
empty lives, lonely lives
carry torch for one who thrives
lonely lives, hollow lives
rooted deep in loneliness
hollow lives, vacant lives
solitary onliness
empty lives, lonely lives

warm-lit windows, love within
seeking warmth, seeking love
on the outside looking in
seeking love, seeking joy
aching heart deprived of hope
seeking joy, seeking touch
void revealed through torchlight's scope
seeking warmth, seeking love

Ronald P. Feldheim

comes the recent cycle 'round
hopeful years, happy years
inroads gained while solace found
happy years, love-filled years
drawn within yet looking out
love-filled years, pain-filled years
love dissolved through fear and doubt
hopeful years, happy years

tearful prayers join prayerful tears
higher ground, coming 'round
Lord, I will NOT cleave to fears
coming 'round, love abounds
your torch carried, hand held high
love abounds, life astounds
bathed in faith I hold Love nigh
higher ground, coming 'round

A TEARDROP

I see the teardrop, caught upon her cheek,
And wonder what transpired within
That but a moment before this glistening jewel
Should fall from her eye.

I see the teardrop, glistening in the sunlight.
I find within every color I have ever known:
The emerald of the grass and trees, the ruby of the
  hibiscus,
The whites and grays and sapphires of the heavens.

I see the teardrop, stopped in mid-cascade.
If I move my head just so
An explosion of light fills my eyes
As the sun shouts God's Glory.

I see the teardrop, and try to fathom its cause.
Was it joy or sorrow, or a confusion of each?
Did I say something wrong, or something right?
Is it a pulling between past and hope, past and fear, past
  and now?

I see the teardrop, and my heart catches,
For, if I am the cause, it can only mean
That I have found a place in her heart
As she has in mine.

Another teardrop wells forth, but this is mine…

Ronald P. Feldheim

DRIVING TO THE SUN

"Look, a Red-headed Woodpecker!", I wanted to say,
But you weren't with me in the car.
The corn fields,
The pecan groves,
The little cypress ponds covered with lily pads…
I needed to share them with you in order to make them
  perfect.
The Jefferson Davis Memorial Highway,
The eye-blink of a spot in the road called Hebron,
The *Southern Living* gardens,
I tried to memorize every inch so I could tell you about them.
Then the sun eased behind a large, black cloud.
The last gift of golden rays sprayed out from behind a
  picotee edge.
I wanted so much to share this with you.
I had developed an armor that allowed me to take in the
  world alone,
To eat its fruit,
Drink its wine,
Capture its sights,
Absorb its places,
And content myself that I could fully enjoy it all.
Now, however, you have penetrated my armor.
Alone is not enough.
Experiencing life in new ways is so much more wonderful
When you are there with me.

Butterflies, Snowbirds, and Passions: Poems and Fantasies

Ronald P. Feldheim

MIRABILE

FLIGHT

ABYSS

SHEKHINAH

YOU

REFLECTION*

The darkness, the darkness creeps in between
The future and the living.
The darkness, the darkness - grim, cold and keen;
It takes, it's never giving.
But you give to me, give again, yet again.
Your light soft suffuses my twilight of pain.
A compass point bearing, my faith to regain.
I'm reflecting you.

I'm drifting, I'm drifting, losing my way.
What is my direction?
I'm drifting, I'm drifting, where did I lay?
A stranger in reflection.
The sun and the moon and the stars know your face;
A comforting beacon, a rainbow in space.
You brighten my world, representing God's grace.
I'm reflecting you.

Ronald P. Feldheim

It's lonely, it's lonely, living apart
Midst teeming populations.
It's lonely, it's lonely, searing my heart;
Trouble with connections.
Then you found a way to illumine my night.
You helped me forge friendships, you make life so bright.
Together in joy this connection so right.
I'm reflecting you.

inspired by Sam Phillips' song Reflecting Light

PASSION*

Seize me, squeeze me,
Such is how you please me.
Softly, firmly,
How your touches burn me.
Such wonder in the night,
How your body feels so right,
As we give each other pleasure in the dawn.
A nip, a kiss, a bite,
Thrusting tongues with sweet delight,
As electric pulses chase away a yawn.

Saying, weighing
What our hearts were praying.
Heaving, cleaving
Bodies interweaving.
My fingers through your hair
As you lay your body bare.
Then, I drink in all your pleasures with desire.
Your sweet lips brush me here
While my tongue will linger there.
Then, our bodies soon erupt with passion's fire.

*inspired by Music of the Night

Ronald P. Feldheim

AND NOT TO YIELD*

O'er yon hill, I yearn to break free
Leaving my fetters behind
Breathe azure sky, wind-dance with a tree
Seeking, myself to find

Long do I wait, weak is my gait
Mourning my agile youth
Anchored by pain, challenging fate
Writing my future truth

Who can I be if I can't be me?
Nature still knows my name
Meadow and wood, blue sky sets me free
Playing the aging game

E'er the wind blows, long the sea rolls
As Ulysses did so do I strive
Ever I seek until my bell tolls
Adventuring sets me alive

*Inspired by Skye Boat Song, and Ulysses by Alfred Lord Tennyson

SOMETIMES YOU WANT TO WALLOW IN YOUR SADNESS

I'm sure glad THAT year is over, they said
Boy, that was a rough year, they said
I hope this year is a better year, they said
As if a year were a tangible thing
As if a year were something we could hold in our hands
As if a year were something we could give back and take a different one, instead

It really WAS a rough year
Suppose I could slice-and-dice it
There were parts I would take out and toss on Mt. Trashmore
There were parts I would remove from my mind
Never to be thought of again
But there were also times that elevated my spirit
There was a time that took me out of myself to an unknown place
And left tears streaking down my face from a joy I have never known
Speechless, blubbering incoherently
I cannot break up the year, though
I cannot take the good bits and delete the rest
I cannot even pretend the miseries never happened, as I am still recovering from them

Ronald P. Feldheim

That year is a single, indivisible, intangible, invisible
  whatever-it-is
I get all of it, or I get none of it, so I took it all
So I have it still, even though it is over

THAT year was the year I got cancer
I was never going to get cancer, but I got cancer
It was a tiny little thing, but it was in the back of my eye
It had to come out, NOW, the doctor said
So the tumor came out, and so did the cloudy lens,
And now, with a miraculous new lens
I can see oh so clearly
I am a survivor

THAT year was also the year I had to have my hip replaced
Congenital dysplasia, the doctor said
I was never going to get my hip replaced, but I got my hip
  replaced
The pain was the determining factor
I endured it as long as I could, until I couldn't
I am becoming bionic

THAT year was the year of the evacuation
Two days in Hell's own traffic jam
And that damned storm kept her eye on us and followed
  us all the way to Tennessee
And hit us where we hid

But while there we passed time in Nashville and
  Chattanooga
And that was fun
But it was followed by two more days in traffic
And that was not fun

THAT year was also the year of the big total solar eclipse
On my lady's birthday
For a present I gifted her with a total eclipse of the sun
In South Carolina, front row, longest duration
Nice move, right?
Yet, it moved me planes beyond anything I expected
The moon opened a hole in the sun that led to infinity
And it sucked me right in
There aren't words...

THAT year brought some additional gifts to myself
A new car after ten years, all bright and shiny
Replete with bells and whistles
Economical, reliable, fun, and pretty to boot
There is also the new apartment with an even better view
  than I had before
The window wall directs my gaze over the pool, over the
  "recreational corridor"
Over the dunes, over the beach, and over the ocean
To that place of myth where the sun shakes itself free

Ronald P. Feldheim

of the sea
In a spray of golden droplets by morning
And the Moon chases after by night dripping silver
THAT year has taught me to count myself among the
  blessed, after all
But sometimes you want to wallow in your sadness

Ronald P. Feldheim

POEMS FROM
A TIME OF COVID

AT LEAST THE BIRDS ARE STILL FLYING FREE

At least the birds are still flying free
Even if we're not
Pent-up frustration
And no place to vent

I **NEED** to be out in Nature
It keeps me sane
I gaze longingly out the window at the beach
And I can't go there
The beaches are CLOSED!
At least the birds are still flying free

We are ordered to hunker down
Shelter in place
I'd rather hunker up
I need my fresh air and sunshine
I want to go to a park
Where I know there are birds
And butterflies and flowers
And sunshine and shade and, and, and…
But the parks are all closed

City parks? Closed
County parks? Closed
State parks? Closed
Everglades National Park is open, but the entrances are
  closed.
What?

Ronald P. Feldheim

At least the birds are still flying free

We are not bears that hibernate
For months at a time
I have to have fresh air.
Nancy asks, "What about Arch Creek?", a county park
Open! it says online
And the neighboring Enchanted Forest?
Open!
Let's go.
If they are really open
And remain open during the week
They could be my salvation
We get to Arch Creek within the hour. It's closed!
Enchanted Forest Park is closed, too
At least the birds are still flying free

Every day I walk the paved path
That runs up and down the beach behind the dunes
But it's not enough
Passing by all the closed-off beach paths
Through the dunes
How I yearn to step out on the sand
Splash in the ocean surf
Sit in the sun and watch the waves roll in
While the sea breeze refreshes

At night we go out for a stroll
Quiet city

Butterflies, Snowbirds, and Passions: Poems and Fantasies

Ronald P. Feldheim

NOW OR THEN

Yes, I talked to my landlord
It must have been this morning
Or was it yesterday morning?
I remember; it was Friday morning
That was today?
It seems like yesterday
Why do you keep asking me those questions?

You see, there is NOW
And there is WAS
NOW is sequential
WAS is not

Did I send in the tour deposit? Yes
When? In the WAS
I did it. What does it matter when?
Did I talk to my sister? Yep
No, I don't remember when
It was in the WAS
We're talking on the phone NOW
Everything else is in the WAS
I know it happened
I just don't remember when
Stop asking

GIVE ME A POEM

Give me a poem, Oh Lord, I said
Help me express your infinite love
I can give you a poem, God said to me
But it won't be what you expect

Give me a poem, I entreated
Make it tell of hope and promise
Have it lift spirits and stretch minds
Where there is darkness have it light a candle
Where there is a glimmer have it fan the flame
Where there is fire make it come roaring up
Where there is pain make it heal

Give me a poem, I repeated
Make it expressive and rich with meaning
And *Adonai* smiled and said
The words that I give you have never been written
You must work with them and mold them
Breathe them in and exhale them in a new form
Find their fragrance, taste their spice
Feel their texture and their heat
What do they sound like?
What is their color?
Open yourself

Ronald P. Feldheim

I reeled then as synesthesia confounded my senses
I teetered outside and heard the most wondrous symphony
Sunlight cascaded downward in whirls and swirls of sublime tones
A mockingbird was painting its song as rainbows of hues wafted from its beak
I turned toward the garden and was astonished
Each flower had its own flavor
Each honeybee had its unique fragrance
From somewhere I was suddenly bathed in warmth
Followed by tendrils of cool air tickling me

I held onto the door frame for dear life
Not able to move
Hardly able to think except to note what was transpiring
The moment was eternal. A minute? A month?
It gradually came to an end, though
My sense of the world returned to normal
Yet I am left with a new understanding
I wanted a poem and I was shown the world
In all its interconnectedness
In all its inner beauty
It is ours if only we use all of our senses to appreciate it
I asked for a poem and the Creator gave me the universe

ACKNOWLEDGEMENTS

I wish to thank my friend Ricki Dorn for coaxing me to pull my poetry together into a cohesive chapbook. She guided me professionally at several crucial points in the process, as well as suggesting specific corrections, additions, and other edits. This books reflects her contributions. Above all, she convinced me that I had something that others might appreciate. Thank you, Ricki.

I also thank Nancy Kraemer, my partner in life and fellow poet. Nancy provided the inspiration for some of the poems, especially the haiku. Sometimes, we would sit and write together, each producing a poem to fit the occasion. My poem, SAFE, is a good example, one of my favorites.

MEET THE AUTHOR

Ronald Feldheim is retired from a career in laboratory medicine as a clinical microbiologist and specialist in clinical computer applications. Although he holds a Bachelor of Science degree in Biology from the University of Miami and a Master of Science degree in Fisheries Biology from the University of Delaware, he went on to study Medical Technology. He is nationally certified, and licensed in the State of Florida as a medical technologist. He has spent his entire career working in hospital laboratories, including fifteen years as a "road warrior" for a major diagnostic equipment manufacturer. He resides in Miami Beach, and his apartment overlooks the beach and ocean.

Writing poems since high school, he was recently encouraged to pull them together into book form. He is also a writer of essays. Some of his work has been included in newsletters and websites. Ron is a member of the South Florida Writers Association and he received recognition for some of his poetry.

Although his professional career has been in science and technology, being out in nature is the activity that makes him come alive. This includes travel to explore new places. Before moving to Miami Beach, he loved to grow tropical fruits, vegetables, and flowers at his home on the mainland. Ron has a mystical connection with the realms of nature and spirit. He is a devotee and teacher of the work of Edgar Cayce, is a hands-on healer, and has studied Jewish Shamanic Healing.

Ron is a proud father and grandfather. He is an active member of his synagogue and a student of Torah. Ron coined the term *Rational Mystic* to describe himself.

Dear Readers:

I hope you enjoyed this little book, and will consider helping me "spread the word" on social media. Posting a positive review on Amazon would also be appreciated.

I would love to hear from you. You can contact me at MiamiBeachRonnie@gmail.com.

Thank you for your support.

Ron

www.ingramcontent.com/pod-product-compliance
Lightning Source LLC
Chambersburg PA
CBHW050333120526
44592CB00014B/2165